Allow Your Soul To Lead

Volume 2

The Aspects of The Soul
&
The 7 Steps
To Self-Discovery And Healing

A Channeled Text
Healing Series

Cindy Edison

Allow Your Soul to Lead: Volume 2
The Aspects of The Soul & The 7 Steps To Self-Discovery And Healing.
Copyright © 2018 Cindy Edison
ISBN: 9781727022124

Table Of Contents:

WELCOME

Greetings Dear One,

Thank you for seeking out our second volume in the series Allow Your Soul To Lead. We are Josef.

As some of you know, we are a collective consciousness of teachers. We are the same as you, in fact we are aspects of you, you see. We are body-less but mind-full, vibrationally speaking. We kid with you however, not so much.

Our perspective is a bit different than yours in that we are focused from a broader perspective, a wider range if you will, which allows us a view of more. It is a view of everything really, everything meaning everything we choose to focus upon. This is what this series is about, focus, choice and healing.

As we move through this series of books that will be an overview of who you really are as a vibrant being of light, we will assist in the expansion of your view of who you really are so you may experience life on earth as your true self, in essence, your Soul. Each book will add to your repertoire and assist in the expansion of your own awareness to include new things, new opportunities and new perspectives from which to thrive.

These 'snippets' of information we are providing to you in these mini-books, if you will, are just enough to get you started in the quest to know who you are as a Soul. If it feels as if we are focused upon getting you to know who you really are, it's because we are. You see, once you know who you are from within, not with-'out', your perspectives will change therefore creating a different life 'outside', meaning your physical reality will change to reflect the changes you've made on the inside of yourself.

True change happens from the inside out. This is clear and is evidenced by the realities you live. Once you understand on the inside that you are creating your outside, you begin to understand why things are 'happening' and why things are the way they are. Understanding is key to change if this is your desire.

The change we are proposing through these volumes is a change offered from our perspective, you see. It is change offered from the umbrella view vibration. As we stand (figuratively speaking) on the mountain top, we are encouraging you to follow our direction as you walk your path below and our direction is focused from inside of you. We are the door-way out. We speak to you as your Soul.

You are powerful creative beings and you are truly loved. In order to feel and express the love that you are as a Soul, you must understand and know your true power, and the power we speak of is within your heart space. The power of your Soul is eminent within the universe.

As we move through this text, our intention with each book is to expand your view to allow more; to allow your perspective to include a higher vibration and held within the higher vibration is more joy, more peace and more love. As you expand your own vibration, you include more possibilities, you see. You include the possibilities that are held within that vibration. It's as if you are standing in a rain storm and your umbrella diameter spans one foot as opposed to your protection spanning five feet. You simply have more coverage and more possibilities for dryness in this example. In other words, the more you expand, the more opportunities for choice you have.

Once again, we welcome you aboard as we assist in the expansion of humanity to include the "New Earth" vibration.

We are Josef.

PRELUDE TO THE WORK

As we begin our second volume of the Allow Your Soul To Lead series, we'd like to recap for a moment the previous work as it relates to what you are about to learn about yourself as a human being.

You are a multi-dimensional being who has chosen to experience physical life for the purpose of the expansion of not only your own Soul's eternal path but for all of humanity and the universe as well. We understand this may sound like a big job however your job is about you.

As we've explained, your Soul, the God-ness who lives within you and within Everything, is your connection to God and is what allows the One-ness of the Universe. You live in a unified field, as it were; it is a field of unification that exists either inside or outside of your current reality. It is a field of vibration that is allowed or not allowed, all dependent upon your awareness, your choice and of course, your focus. Your focus is your ultimate connection to the discovery of who you really are and is where your choice lies.

So, we've explained up to this point that you are a multi-dimensional being meaning you, aspects of you, exist simultaneously on other vibratory timelines and you have the ability to experience these other realms through your Soul aspects. You are a being who has a Soul aspect, the God-ness of You, an ego aspect who knows the ropes of the third dimensional realm (the realm of the current collective earth plane) and you have a human aspect who is, for lack of a better term, doing the physical living of the "You" of you. In other words, the human aspect is having the physical experience and the rest of your aspects are benefiting from it.

We understand this concept of aspects, different 'parts' of you, may be confusing at times which is why we are dedicating this entire booklet to the subject. Our intention with this information is of course, your expansion, but also to assist in the understanding of the 'big-ness' of you. It is the crux to the knowing of who you really are and how the aspects of you can, if you choose to allow it, assist in your experience in the physical world.

These books are meant to do one thing overall and that is to give you a good idea of the expansive nature of the human aspect which will cause expansion simply by the knowledge of more. When you expand, you again expand your possibilities in all areas, you see. So, by explaining to you the multi-dimensional aspects, it will give you a more clear view of you from the umbrella view from which we teach. When we interact with any of you, we see the larger 'You', you see. We see you for who you truly are and that is our goal with you which is to provide the information so you can get a glimpse of yourself from our perspective which is the perspective of the Soul.

We touched on the aspects in our first book as a beginning point and in order for you to understand the multi-dimensional nature of the human, you need to understand how you are experiencing those other dimensions through the other aspects of yourself. This is key to moving for-ward.

We will say, at this time, this information will be the beginning stages of this concept of living as the aspects of the real you, for as we offer this concept and understanding, it will evolve on its own as does everything. So, as we begin to reveal more about You, to you, you will begin to ask more about you and the momentum will begin rolling down the road of wisdom and understanding for we are encouragers of questions and curiosity where you are concerned, for the more you know, the more you want to know.

As these new doorways present themselves, we encourage you to walk through them with us as we all expand together.

Aspect: Your Soul has many aspects of itself, each on different time-lines. There is no vibrational death so to speak, only the transformation of energy. When the physical body is no longer needed for the Soul's expansion, it is transformed to a different energy vibration. It remains as energy.

You have experienced many physical lifetimes, some longer in years than others however the length of the physical life is not a component to the Soul's experience. The Soul comes with purpose, lives with purpose and the purpose is always inclusive of expansion of itself as the love vibration. There is no end, no finish line to this. Your timeframe is eternal. This is what our friends, Abraham, meant when they taught, "you cannot get it wrong and you never get it done." This truth is an eternal truth and all aspects of you, as an individual Soul, live on, existing on other time-lines where their focus lies, all of different vibrations yet all connected to the One.

This is how we introduced the term Aspect in the introductory book. Our partner would like to include her simplified version of how to understand the word 'aspect' and that is as a slice of pie. The whole pie, for in-stance, makes up God - Source - The All. Each slice, however thin, is comprised of everything contained in its Source and has the same flavor. It has the same power.

Your Soul is a slice of God and you are a slice of your Soul. All are as powerful as the Whole and the Whole is not complete without each slice. We like this analogy, too.

In this volume, we will concentrate on the three aspects that are impacting you the most as you live your physical life on your planet. As you come to understand more and more about how these three aspects interact, you will be on your way to your New Earth Vibration.

OVERVIEW

We would like to begin talking about the aspects in analogy form for better understanding. The analogy we are choosing is that of an orchestra. In this scenario, your Soul is the orchestra, the human aspect is the conductor and the instruments are the coordinating aspects. Each instrument carries a different tone, or vibration, and when they all work together and are in tune, the manifestation is joyful sound vibration and each instrument is in alignment.

However, if one instrument is out of tune let's say, there is discord and it is up to the conductor to realign that instrument so it is back in key with the rest of the piece that is being played, which in this case, is your physical reality.

If you were to think about the 'all' of you, from our perspective, you would see all of you meaning the Soul's journey...the 'all' of your individual and collective journey. 'You' would include all your experiences spanning all timelines, all incarnations and all those 'spaces' in between your physical experiences.

The 'you', meaning your consciousness, at any given time is ever expanding and this expansion happens and evolves through the aspects of you. The aspects who are simultaneously living - existing - experiencing - other vibrational timelines that are manifestations of the matching consciousness vibration. We are not trying to confuse you although sometimes it may seem that way however what we are intending is an overview of the expansive nature of who you really are.

Aspects are pieces of you. They are the make up of your personality. They are the passion of you. They are the analytic side of you. They are the creative side of you. They are the manifestation of the purpose of your Soul. You see, as your Soul evolves and makes choices in order to evolve itself in and through the love vibration, when those choices are 'being formulated' so to speak, what manifests are the aspects. The aspects then carry out the experiences to benefit not only the Soul's expansion, but as the Soul benefits through this expansion, so does every other aspect along with it. This is how the Soul in its entirety (which includes the universe as well) expands. You might say it is a collective agreement to evolve.

This is a big subject and one that we will delve into more and more as this message evolves but for this series, we will discuss and explain the benefit to you, the human aspect of you, as to how it relates to the hu-man experience of your Soul.

As the human aspect experiences the physical world, it has come with a purpose which is the purpose of the Soul. No one can tell you what your true purpose is although they can assist in your opening up to the revelation of it. Your Soul, if focused upon and 'allowed', will lead you through experiences that will unfold its purpose as you are living your physical life.

The human aspect, as we've referred to it in the first book, is the "ground crew" so to speak. Its purpose and intention is to experience the contrast of the third dimension in order to expand not only its consciousness but the consciousness of the Soul and universe simultaneously. There is no separation of any of these 'parts' you see. All aspects are orchestrated in order to give the human aspect the assistance it needs in order to live out the purpose for which it came.

For instance, you may be a 'creative type' as our human friends describe those who have 'vision' and can physically create whether through voice, instrument, paint, carpentry, etc. They contain a strong creative aspect and when they are in the creative mode as you say, they are assisted by their creative aspect who brings with it all the creativity from the creative experiences it has had on the eternal scale and it lends those vibrations to the human aspect and they co-create whatever it is they choose. The creative aspect in a sense lends itself to the human aspect and they work together to expand. It is a co-creation from alignment with their Soul Through this co-creation, the Soul expands as well. This is how the aspects and the human aspect co-create for the Soul.

When the aspects are in alignment with the Soul, they are as the orchestra, all playing in sync in order to manifest the overall purpose.

THE HUMAN ASPECT

As we've discussed, of the many aspects of the 'you' of your Soul, the human aspect is the aspect that is currently experiencing the physical world of the third dimensional realm of earth.

At this time, and as some of you are aware, the earth has ascended meaning the vibration of the earth itself has risen in consciousness. Be-cause the earth is a living, breathing being, it shifts its consciousness as well and that shift has been occurring for many, many years. This is the shift toward, what is sometimes referred to as, The New Earth. The ascension has taken place and the vibration of the earth has risen above that of the third dimensional realm. What this means is the conscious-ness of the earth itself is no longer a match to the fear based realm of the third dimension.

As the human population is currently in the process of shifting from a fear based collective consciousness to that of the Soul, the opportunities are extended to all human aspects to choose love over fear in each moment from an intensified love vibration. As more and more choose the Soul's perspective over that of the ego, the collective consciousness shifts to reflect those choices. The time is now to choose to ascend or not. Those who choose to stay in the momentum of the ego will continue to experience fear based lives and as more and more choose the love vibration, the collective consciousness of fear-based thoughts 'shrinks', however it still remains intact and as destructive and in fact, continues to get more intense.

The 'human' that you are in this physical lifetime is the 'human' you've always been, meaning - you, as the human aspect - are an ongoing evolution of the vibration you choose as you live your physical life. Simply put, you are who you always are, only an evolved version of you. Each time you visit the physical experience, you retain or take with you all your experiences in love, in the expanded version, and you continue on your eternal journey in alignment with your Soul.

So, when the Soul decides to incarnate, it chooses the time, place, parents, etc., all of which are important for Its purpose. All is choice. Always. All is chosen vibrationally and when the Soul makes these choices, they are made from the Soul's perspective of the pure, positive love vibration and all the components that are lined up to ensure the Soul's purpose is accomplished, are based in the love vibration as well. This means all those who are in your Soul family, so to speak, and all those who have signed up with you to assist you along your path, have one thing in common and that is the intention of the expansion of the collective vibration of love. The Soul sets its intention to not only expand itself but to manifest a physical experience of peace, joy and love in abundance, un-til it overflows. It is the human aspect's choosing outside of alignment that throws the human off course.

Through the human aspect's physical experience, the Soul expands as does the Universe with each choice of love based experiences the hu-man aspect chooses along the way. In each choice, the opportunity to choose a matching vibration then exists for the next choice. As the hu-man aspect chooses its way through the physical journey, it creates a vibrational road map of sorts in which to follow. This map either takes them toward love or toward fear. It is in the choosing that all manifestations are set in motion.

The human aspect is an extension of not only the Soul aspect and the ego aspect but all aspects that exist on other simultaneous timelines. Until now, the human aspect's vibration was not in a position to seek assistance from its other aspects in that the collective vibration of the third dimension was riddled in fear. It is because of the earth's rising and simultaneous rising of the earth's consciousness that the human awareness 'levels' are able to achieve a higher light, a higher vibrational pathway. This pathway includes access to other timelines and other aspects.

Not all aspects are of a higher vibration, yet all are accessible through focus. They are simply different. For example, the vibration of the human collective one hundred years ago did not include the opportunities that are available today simply because of the evolutionary status, or aware-ness, of the human at that time. Each generation comes in with the additional vibratory patterns that have been established by the generation before it. This is event driven evolution. This evolutionary manifestation is not based on the time on the planet but the timing of the planet, you see. It is the evolution of the All that is in play in this scenario.

So as the human aspect evolves through all its aspects, all -collective aspects evolve as well. At this time, the human aspect is being given a wider range from which to choose. It is the choosing of higher vibrational living that is currently in front of you. As the human aspect has a higher understanding of who it really is in relationship to its Source, or its Soul, the opportunities for understanding and therefore expansion increase as well.

THE HUMAN - EGO ASPECT RELATIONSHIP

We will begin this section by describing how the aspects that are pertinent to the human aspect's experience in the third dimension play a role in the reality that is created. Specifically, we will discuss in more detail how the human aspect and the ego aspect co-mingle their experiences in this physical lifetime and those on other timelines.

The human aspect is comprised of not only the Soul aspect (as we are for Cindy) but the ego aspect as well. These are the three most focused upon during the physical experience up to this point in your time. As we said before, the vibration of your planet, or the planet's 'awareness' has expanded therefore offering more opportunities from which to choose for all those who inhabit her. This level of vibration, as we stated, has not been reached before and is the natural evolution of any being. As the earth ascends, all who are connected to her have the option to ascend as well. This may be viewed or yes, experienced, as 'being in the flow.'

Our partner is asking now what happens to those who choose not to ascend with the earth? We say that all vibration that has ever existed will continue to exist. What is before you now is an opportunity for a collective expansion by way of the individual inhabitants, mainly the human population. Prior to this shift in consciousness, the 'ground' was not pre-pared as in the earth's vibration you see. Therefore, as the ground has risen, so to speak, those who are entwined with the 'ground' are offered the opportunity to expand vibrationally as well.

As for those who are not allowing the consciousness, not allowing or not believing in anything other than what they have experienced, or not, up to this point, they will remain in the denseness of the earth's lower realm. We are confusing Cindy a bit so let us see if we can clear this up...

Just as a human has the ability to raise his or her vibration and still live within the third dimensional realm on the earth plane but create different realities based on their vibration, the earth has the same ability and capability you see. As the vibration of the earth continues to rise, it expands the opportunities not only for herself but for the collective that she holds, so to speak. In other words, when her awareness is expanded, it expands for the All as when your awareness expands it not only affects you but the All as well. But that does not mean if you choose not to ascend at this time that you will cease to exist! It does however mean that you have more opportunity vibrationally to create a peaceful, joyful life for yourself and for others simply by your own expansion into what is now available. The same is true for the earth as well.

So, if one chooses (and there will be many) not to ascend at this time, that does not mean they will never ascend for all, eventually, will allow the movement. However, they will remain in a 'darker' space meaning there will be less light you see, for the light is the manifestation of the higher vibration and when the higher vibration ascends through the individuals and becomes the 'new' collective consciousness, it will not be as easily accessible by those who are not interested for whatever reason because they will live in more denseness and it will be a larger 'jump' out. Our partner is asking us for an analogy and we will offer one now.

Picture two people, one who lives in a lower vibration of fear and one who lives in a higher vibration of love. They have very different experiences although they both live in the earth plane where their physical reality is focused. The fearful, limited thinker will live a life of struggle emotionally and physically because their vibration is not in alignment with who they really are which is their Soul aspect. The struggle will begin internally which will create a physical manifestation of their insides so to speak. We are not speaking necessarily about financial means however that, most likely, will follow suit. Fear based living effects all areas of the physical life experience.

On the other hand, the one who understands how their reality is created, will live the vibration they carry as well, which is, as some refer to as being 'up in the clouds' meaning whatever denseness, whatever darkness, whatever negative energy will be below their field of vision, their field of awareness, and therefore not accessible unless they drop their own vibration to include it in their current awareness. If you think about this in terms of an elevator, you are either in the basement or the penthouse and all floors in between are of your choosing.

As we were saying before, the three aspects we are focusing on in this writing are the Soul, the human and the ego. We want to interject here for a moment and say Cindy is a fan of the capitalized 'Soul' as this is a statement of respect from her. We appreciate her sentiments but it's not a requirement we have imposed. We respect her choice. But we digress.

THE MULTI-DIMENSIONAL YOU

When we discuss the aspects of a Soul, it is a foreign subject to most people for they are not aware, first of all, that they are multi-dimensional which means you have the ability to experience other realms of vibration, other realms of energy. These vibratory realms are the other dimensions, meaning they are vibrationally based and can be experienced by anyone who comes into vibrational agreement with them.

The earth plane has existed in the third dimension for eons. It has and continues to shift on its own, as it naturally 'shakes off' the dense vibrations that keep her 'down'. All things evolve and of course, this includes the earth body. She is a living being as well that holds a vibration of her own. However, she too is effected by her inhabitants as we touched on in the first book, and the collective vibration, specifically of humanity, plays a role in her existence and her momentum as well. We would liken the denseness of the collective vibration of fear of humanity as the mon-key on her back.

The earth plane's third dimension, as it rises to a higher vibration, will remain as all energy remains, focused upon or not, in the dense field and all those who have or are rising will rise with her, collectively. This is the shift that is currently happening in the human realm of operation, shifting from the third dimension to the fifth dimensional realm. This is the opportunity that is available to all at this time.

You see, as you raise your vibration, you experience new realms of being. You expand your consciousness and your awareness which includes the expansion of and inclusion of the opportunities and possibilities that exist in the higher realms of consciousness and this is where your New Earth is already existing.

The term 'multi-dimensional' is confusing to most of our human friends because it has not been taught and is not widely understood. However, it is who you are from the broader perspective, the Soul's perspective.

There are unlimited dimensions of reality, all existing as vibratory patterns. We will explain it as it relates to the human experience as best we can and in a way, it will benefit the human physical experience as it is introduced into your field of consciousness. In other words, once it comes into your awareness, you have the choice to benefit from the knowledge. It is another piece to who you really are.

ASPECTS AND TIMELINES

The aspects of you are all currently having their own experience as you as a human aspect at this time are having yours in the third dimensional realm. This was your choice of realms of experience for your Soul's purpose at this particular time, and what a time it is to be on this earth during this consciousness shift that is occurring. Each aspect of you, as we have stated, is vibrating at a different frequency therefore existing on a different timeline, one with the vibratory pattern that is matching the vibration of that particular aspect.

The dimensions are 'places' where timelines take you, meaning the awareness that the vibrational pattern matches includes all opportunities on the matching timeline. We do not want to confuse so we will use an analogy here to make our point and expand your awareness simultaneously.

Let's picture a timeline as a highway of sorts. As you are on any particular highway, you have many options along the highway to experience, all of matching vibration. One highway might take you to a big city where excitement and many others abound. Another highway may be taking you around a mountain, above the trees into the snow where there are only scatters of others along the route. The opportunities of experience on each highway are different depending on the path you are currently choosing, choosing vibrationally.

There are many timelines that are available, for the timelines are chosen by you, regardless of where you 'are' meaning you can be of the earth plane and experience other timelines through the adjusting of your vibration, you see. The timelines have little to do with your physicalness but are vibrationally experienced.

Our partner has experienced what have been labeled 'past lives' through the adjusting of her vibration and the desire to experience what another aspect of her Soul is currently experiencing. We would like to touch on these labels, past lives, future lives, etc. for a moment to offer some clarity.

As we've said, there is no 'time' in this message, for our 'timing' ... 'your' timing is vibrationally based and is available for your participation at any time. The eternal life your Soul is experiencing is all happening now. There is, in truth, no past or future for all in the universe is happening and is accessible now.

As for your participating in it, you are always participating. You are a vibrational being before anything else. You are participating whether you are focused on your vibration or not which is why we are encouraging the understanding and focus of your own vibration for it is the key to everything you experience.

Vibrational timing is what causes manifestation and manifestation comes through vibrational agreement. There is no time as you know it. All, what you call past or future, lives are happening now on other timelines based on their vibration. Timelines are chosen through your agreement with the vibration of a particular timeline. We will use one of our partner's experiences to demonstrate the power of timeline experiences.

Cindy is giving us the go ahead with this personal information knowing the healing that is available through this exercise as it was for her and she hopes it will assist others as well. She will tell you her story.

"I had been searching for a healing that would, in essence, wipe out the experiences of my childhood, like many of us have. The details don't matter for this story, only that it involved my father and is not unlike so many others who have experienced what I call leftovers that I can't seem to shake. Mine had to do with my worthiness and value. His teaching to me plagued every area of my life and I found it difficult to let it go, even with all the understanding I had from my Guides. It just wasn't enough.

One morning during meditation, I decided to seek another avenue, another timeline if you will, so I called on the vibration of Archangel Michael to assist me on this journey. He willingly and lovingly stepped forward and we began to walk together. We were moving to a different timeline and he was taking me, as requested, to where the issue began with my father. I figured I would understand if I could see what caused it in the first place.

Keep in mind I have an understanding of Soul families and Soul contracts and I know my father is a Soul traveler with me and we have played many roles for each other on other timelines so this request was nothing new to my way of thinking.

As we walked, it was dark but not frightening. At one point, I remember looking up at him and saying, "I'm so tired" and he picked me up and carried me. I'm not sure what this has to do with the experience but I assume the vibration was so different, it made me tired as I was feeling my own shift to a more dense vibration.

When we stopped and he put me down beside him, we were in front of what looked like a stage and there was an old shack in front of us. The scene inside was of a young man standing over a young woman in rags who was lying on the floor in the fetal position and the man was beating her. I knew she was me and he was my father. We were married on this timeline and he was yelling condescendingly, telling me I was not worth anything and I had ruined his life. She lay there motionless with her hands over her face and he was raging.

I looked up at Michael and he said, "His rage is not about you. He is only releasing his own pain, from his own experience, toward you. It has nothing to do with you."

"I've seen enough. Let's go" I said, and I began to turn around. He stopped me and said, "No, we must fix this first."

As I turned back around, the scene on the inside now was the young man sitting at the table, head in his hands, and he was sobbing. The young woman was standing behind him, comforting and loving him. I looked up at Michael and he said, "now this ending vibration has changed. It has not only healed you from this experience but it has healed him as well."

We thank our partner for sharing this experience and we will continue and explain what transpired for her.

You see, when a vibration is left for any reason, as in the ego's participation with the Soul in the earth experience when the Soul transitions, the ending vibration, the last vibration that is acknowledged (or focused upon), is where the vibration remains in its dormancy until it is again focused upon. So, in relation to Cindy's experience in returning to the beginning timeline of this vibration that has carried through on many timelines, since the vibration was never changed within her or him, the manifestations of that vibration continued as well. The momentum carried on, you see.

Upon her return to that timeline, she, with the assistance of the higher vibration of Archangel Michael, was able to change the outcome of that vibrational pattern by experiencing an outcome from the Soul's perspective as opposed to that of the ego. Not only did the vibration shift for her but for him as well for the experience was the factor and the experience is what carried that vibration. Now that the ending of that experience has been 're-experienced' so to speak, the momentum has been re-directed and the awareness of that aspect of her on that timeline has expanded and is no longer subject to the lower vibratory pattern of that timeline.

Another note to this experience. Cindy's father in this current lifetime, transitioned into non-physical over twenty-five years ago from this earthly plane. However, her re-experiencing benefits him as well as his Soul moves forward, too. The experience has shifted. The vibration of the experience has shifted onto a new timeline for all involved.

The power that you hold through your vibrational awareness is unlimited. It is through the ever-evolving wisdom and knowledge of your Soul, of who you really are, that you expand to experience the fullness of the Oneness of God.

ASPECT HEALING

You are energy. Every part of your physical body is energy. Your Soul, the eternal larger part of you is pure energy vibration. The 'physical you' is the physically manifested rendition of your Soul's energy.

All manifestations are a result of vibrational agreement meaning the vibration you are emitting at any given time is being matched by the Universal Law of Attraction. This is how everything is created, through vibrational agreement.

You are either manifesting as a result of vibrational alignment with your Soul and the manifestations are joyful, loving and abundant, or your manifestations are the result of your misalignment and are fear based. In this earthly plane, that would be illness, physical and emotional pain and any emotion that is not of love. These are signs of your vibrational agreement with the presented thoughts of the ego.

You are always manifesting and the life you are living is a manifestation of your current vibration. When there is a manifestation that is not to your liking, it is an indication that you are out of alignment with your source, the Soul's natural vibration of love.

As your aspects are having their experiences, namely the human aspect who has visited this earth plane many times, there are instances when the human aspect is left 'holding the bag' as it were. This bag would contain within it those manifestations of the choices (the vibrations) that were out of alignment as the Soul takes with it only those choices that were in alignment and aligned with love. The choices and manifestations that were in alignment you see are all emotionally based. They are manifestations of expansion of love. This is what the Soul's purpose is and what it takes with it as it transitions and focuses elsewhere. When we say, 'takes with it' we mean vibrationally. The Soul expands with each choice of love and it 'takes with it' the expanded version of itself.

As for the human aspect, it is an ongoing evolution of the aspect of the Soul who is the earth plane visitor, so to speak. It is always the vibrational match to where it left off, as it lies dormant between incarnations. The vibrational body remains as the vibration that it was when the Soul removed its focus and when the Soul returns to the body of the human aspect, it brings with it all the expansion it has gained since it's last term of focus. That is the simple explanation.

This is where Aspect Healing comes in. If the human aspect is left with something out of alignment emotionally, when the Soul returns, although the Soul has expanded, the human aspect has not. Until it gets 'back in touch' with its Soul aspect in the current vibration of the earth plane, it is returning to the earth plane knowing what it experienced before which is why we teach Allow Your Soul To Lead. By doing this and assisting the Soul to live out its physically focused purpose on earth, the human aspect benefits from the Soul's expansion. The Soul is the Guide for the human aspect in this regard as well.

It doesn't matter what, where or when the misalignment occurred, only that it did. The only action necessary is to return the aspect to its original form of alignment with its Source, or its Soul.

The experience our partner Cindy provided serves as the example for this healing. She chose to do it through meditation. At that time, she had a strong meditation practice so it was the path of least resistance for her. Others may choose meditation and others may choose the help of an experienced teacher or energy healer, as they are sometimes referred to. We would like to add our term for this modality and that would be 'aspect aligner". They, in a sense, are assisting in the realigning of the misaligned aspect energy. It matters not how the healing is initiated but it is completed through the focus and desire of the seeker.

A key element to this type of healing is belief. If there is belief that all things are possible through the movement of energy, this healing will work. If there is doubt in the process and doubt in the expectation to the degree that the momentum the doubt carries overrides that of the Soul's knowing, the healing will not work. Those who perform and assist in the healing of the aspect are not key, other than their holding of the healing light of the energy within the realm of the seeker but the seeker must allow the healing as in anything else that is a desired manifestation.

THE STEPS TO HEALING

Although there are many types of healing and many desires for different types of healing including physical and emotional, there is one source of all pain whether physical or emotional and that is skewed vibrational alignment.

When any aspect, namely the human aspect and/or the ego aspect as the focus on this volume, is out of alignment with the Soul aspect, there is discord in the body which includes the mind of the human. This is the cause of all ailment. This is the cause of addiction; as some would deem it the 'root' cause. It is where it begins and soon the manifestation occurs either mentally and/or physically. Until the aspect is brought into alignment and out of the fear-based vibration, the manifestations will continue in some form or another.

Specifically, where addiction is concerned, up until this point in time, there has been a twelve-step program that was put into place in your year of 1939. It has helped many and it has failed many because each individual has a different vibrational make up and although some would prefer all programs to work the same for all those who embark, you are individuals who could not be more different vibrationally, one from the other. When a consensus is taken, the majority of those who agree with whatever is on the dominant side, win. Unfortunately for the others who may disagree for whatever reason, they are deemed losers in the polls. In other words, they are those who 'don't fit in'.

The collective consciousness of your planet, up until this point in time, has been one of fear based beliefs and rituals. From organized religions to atheism, the collective, generally speaking, is more apt to agree with those who appear to know more or speak more loudly so the bandwagon is built and many jump on as it carries the crowd to the town square, so to speak, and from that crowd, groups are formed and the like-minded thought is the dominant vibration regardless of what the thinking is. Consequently, anyone who bucks the system is labeled troublemaker or 'weird' or 'oddball out', however those who stand outside the crowd and do their own thing are those who usually bring innovation and healing to the crowds who are judging others and building courthouses and jails for all those who don't agree with them.

Now we are not advocating the breaking of your laws for your system is built on laws and structures that you believed were necessary, however this 'necessity' too stems from skewed alignment and fear.

It is the individual who must first come to understand and discover who they really are and from that alignment, others will follow but this following is a vibrational leading, it's a choice, and it is set by example, not by words. It is a vibrational agreement you see, because like attracts like and the Universal Law of Vibrational Attraction never fails.

If you were to look within your groups of those who claim to agree, you would find many who would justify their agreement by adding their individual thoughts and beliefs and making the agreement their own but usually in their own mind, for if they were to speak their own thinking into their group, they would be, in some cases, banned and bullied simply for thinking differently than the others. So, they sit quietly and stew, out of alignment with who they truly are, just to be outwardly accepted by others. It is through this desire for outside acceptance that the manifestation of their misalignment begins and the momentum starts, poised in the opposite direction from the Soul's alignment. It is in this illusion of separation that the human aspect creates the discord that leads to illness through the path of least resistance. The result is mental anguish and physical ailment and we say unless and until the vibration is aligned back with its Source, the manifestations will continue to expose the misalignment of vibration.

The current vibration of your planet, as we have previously noted, is at a level now, more expansive than ever before because of the momentum that has been set in motion where the human aspect is given the opportunity to choose a higher vibrationally based discovery of themselves. It is at a place where healing is available to all through their own power and this power is in the knowing of who they are. That is not to say the power has not always been within you, however because of the expansive nature of your current collective vibration and the desire set forth by the masses, it is more available to those who are seeking.

Your planet is in a healing mode, if you will. It is availing itself to its inhabitants and as your planet is in the process of healing itself, the human population is afforded that healing energy in much larger doses than ever before.

As your planet continues to expand its own vibration of love, the energy - the vibration of that expansion - is more readily available as we said. You, too, are in the healing mode as well which is the reason and the purpose for this text. This is a healing series that is being brought into your energetic field for one purpose and that is to offer an alternative way to heal yourself therefore healing others along your way. As each heals, all heal and the collective consciousness of your world simultaneously lifts itself, ultimately, above the denseness of the third dimension. You are lifting yourselves out of the dark, so to speak.

As you continue to move and build that momentum, the healing that is necessary is desired in many areas of your population. It spans from hunger, to poverty, to addiction to loneliness and to your view of death on your planet. All these 'ailments' are manifestations of the vibration of fear and the illusion of separation from your Source. We use the word illusion because you can never - never can you be - separate from your Source, you see. But this lie has resulted in what you are living today. It is a lie that has run rampant throughout your history and it has condescendingly slapped humanity in the face. Our partner is cringing a bit with the use of this analogy however from our perspective, your Soul's perspective, it is, in a word, lunacy.

As you are recognizing and will recognize more and more as we move forward, we are not shy with our use of your language and we are direct. There is not time for dilly dallying anymore for the time is upon us now. We are offering our human friends a different perspective with which to see their own light and as this one light - your light - is shining, other lights will follow. Now is the opportunity to shine. We suggest you engage and seek to understand yourself and to discover who you truly are. This is the current flow of your world at a higher level of vibration; it is a level available to all who seek it but you must seek it for yourselves.

We are introducing now our version of the twelve steps to recovery. It is the version put forth by your Soul's perspective. It is the perspective of God, if you prefer that term, and it is the perspective of All that Is. It is grounded in self-responsibility, self-love and choice. It is for the individual and the group. It is contingent on nothing outside of itself and is meant to assist in the healing of your world at its current and ever expanding vibrational pattern.

Our partner would like to include this quote at this time and we agree it is fitting. "Even if you're on the right track, you'll get run over if you just sit there." - Will Rogers.

We like this thought and we think it demonstrates what we are saying here. Everything is evolving. The Universal vibration is never resting for it is in constant motion forward. As the vibration of your planet increases and expands, it goes faster meaning the momentum increases as the boulder rolling downhill. Now is the opportunity to release your oars, so to speak, and 'go with the flow."

Following are what we are offering as the evolved version of your twelve-step recovery program, however our steps are meant to include all those in need of healing of any kind, not only addiction. These steps are based on Universal laws with which you fit whether you recognize it or not. However, once you recognize and acknowledge your place in the Universe and how you 'fit in' which is the recognition of who you really are, your journey is an enjoyable experience, chosen consciously and joyfully and it is experienced in abundance, until if overflows.

THE 7 STEPS OF SELF DISCOVERY AND HEALING

1) I am the creator of my own reality and the higher power I seek is within me.

2) I have the power within me to restore and heal my thoughts and my body to its original form and purpose for being;

3) I acknowledge that each decision I make is of my own free will and my own choice and I alone am responsible for the creation of all manifestations in my life;

4) Through my own discovery of who I really am and through the acknowledgment of my eternal nature, I understand there is no wrong, there is only vibrationally chosen experiences which always lead me to more opportunities for choosing.

5) In each moment, I have the ability to choose differently. As long as there is choice, there is hope and there is always choice.

6) In each moment, I am the perfect manifestation of my choices and I carry within me the opportunity to manifest myself mentally and physically in any way I choose.

7) I am an aspect of God. My inherent vibration is the healing vibration of pure love and is accessible to me through my focus upon it. As my awareness of who I really am expands, all things are possible.

These steps are a compilation of what was introduced in Volume One of the Allow Your Soul To Lead Series so, in essence, this is a book in review as it pertains to the healing of the human aspect.

Now we will expand on each step, one by one.

1) I am the creator of my own reality and the higher power I seek is within me.

You are the creator of your own reality whether you choose to believe it or acknowledge it outwardly or not. Your reality, externally lived or internally experienced in your body, is a direct reflection of your vibration; it is the manifestation of your internal vibration expressed in the physical world. As you are an expression of the vibration of your Soul that manifested you, the existence you create is the expression of the vibration held and emitted from within you.

If you are carrying a dominant vibration of fear, you are living a life of negative emotion that is a low vibration, resulting in struggle (emotional and/or physical), confusion, hardship and the like. In other words, your vibration is in a state of unrest and is evidenced by your outward living circumstances. Once your vibration is adjusted internally and streamlined into alignment with that of your Soul, your outward reality adjusts as well to match the manifestation of its current alignment.

The power to align or to go askew is held within you and is expressed through the choices you make. The free will that is inherent within you is the will of choice. It is the power of change and when that power is put into motion, so to speak, change occurs. The power is your vibration and your vibration is controlled by your choices. It is an intimate relationship with your Soul and is found within your consciousness. It is not outside of you for if you are seeking a "God" outside of yourself, you are seeking an illusory being manipulated by the fear vibration.

Your vibration is the key to all change. It is the Universal magnet and you are the connecting point. All power is within you and is the means to expression for the purpose of growth and expansion. This power is fueled by you or suppressed by you. However, you choose to use it is up to you and you will manifest all of your vibrational choices. It is law.

2) I have the power within me to restore and heal my thoughts and my body to its original form and purpose of being.

The power of change, whether it be a new desire or a restoration and healing of an existing circumstance, is found within your vibration. Your vibration is in constant magnetic motion, calling its counterpart to it at all times. It calls out to the Source of its being and your Source responds immediately by sending the matching vibration that is, as far as your Source is concerned, being requested. This is the true meaning of Jesus' words, "Ask and it is given." He was speaking vibrationally about the Universal Law of Attraction. It does not fail itself.

If your desire is for healing in any way, whether it be from an addiction or the holding of too much physical weight, the first step is a shift in vibration. This shift begins with a thought of choice, perhaps a shift in perspective, and the momentum that creates the shift then begins and will continue along this path as long as the thought vibrations coming from you are matching those before them. In other words, if you are consciously choosing loving thoughts, you are building the momentum toward your Soul's perspective. If you begin by choosing loving thoughts and then shift to choosing fearful thoughts along your way, your vibration will reflect the uneasiness of your path and your manifestations will be, in a word, confused.

When you are not experiencing what you prefer, the first place to look is at your thoughts and the vibrations you are putting out to the Universe. What you are living and what you are thinking always match. No exceptions.

As the Universe matches more and more like thoughts to those that are being emitted through their vibratory pattern, the vibration of the new chosen thoughts begins to manifest into your reality whether it is relief from an addiction or a different perspective or your physical vehicle. Whatever the case, it matters not what 'is' at this moment. As our dear friends Abraham teach, 'what is, is old news' meaning what 'is' is a manifestation of thought. To create a new manifestation, you must emit a new vibration formed from new thoughts.

In order to restore alignment to that of your Soul, or your original form which is pure love vibration, you must first choose the change. You must choose the Soul's perspective as opposed to the thoughts your ego is presenting along the way. You must be cognizant of your thinking and the patterns you are allowing for these patterns are your indication of what is to come in your physical reality. There is no way around this for the Universal laws are ever present and working in each moment whether you are consciously choosing your vibration or not.

3) I acknowledge that each decision I make is of my own free will and my own choice and I alone am responsible for the creation of all manifestations in my life.

Your free will is in your ability to choose. No one can choose your vibration for you although they can make choices for you by your consent. Choosing something outside of yourself and choosing your vibration are two different things. When you choose your vibration, it is a conscious choosing of thought.

Regardless of what others may think or influence into you, you are still responsible for your own vibration. It is your responsibility to yourself to take control of your thoughts for this is where your true power lies; it is your eternal point of creation. It is yours and yours alone.

When you give your power over to someone or some 'thing', it is also of your choosing. If you believe you do not have choice, you are in vibrational agreement with the ego's presentation of fear. This is fear of self-responsibility because choice always exists. You are always choosing vibrationally which is the part you play in the Universal Law of Attraction. You emit, whether consciously or by default, and the Universal magnet connects to your vibration and the manifestation takes place.

4) Through my own discovery of who I really am and through the acknowledgment of my eternal nature, I understand there is no wrong, there is only vibrationally chosen experiences which always lead me to more opportunities for choosing.

Our predecessor, Abraham, teaches "You cannot get it wrong and you never get it done" and this statement of eternal truth plays well with our fourth step, for you are eternal beings.

The Soul of you, the God within you, is a continuum of vibrational love energy and it moves through the universe, constantly choosing its next experience based on its intention, its vibrational intention of expansion. Through this opening up or expansion of your awareness of the truth of who you are, you begin to create, through your own vibration, experiences that will lead you toward more and more opportunities to choose. You choose your way through eternity, you see. You choose and each choice leads you down your path. There is no wrong path and there is no 'waste' of time for time is an illusion of your earthly realm. We say illusion because in the scheme of things where your Soul's purpose is concerned, time is not of the essence. Time does not exist. Your Soul's experiences are based in timing and manifestation so Abraham's words, "you never get it done" serve this step well.

As you continue to open up or as some deem it, awaken, you begin to discover on your own - not by the likes of an outdated book or by the words of someone before you, but by your own vibrational discovery of who you are, your true self that will emerge and your physical life will reflect this awakening by way of experiences that match it. You will begin to make choices based on your own Soul's knowing through the understanding of the ego's presentation of contrast and the physical and emotional manifestations that accompany it.

Your true journey is one of self-discovery. There is no experience, no feeling, no choice that is not part of that journey for all experiential learning is valuable to the Soul. It is the, as Abraham would say, closing of the gap between your ego's thoughts and those of your Soul. That is the journey, my friend. It is the moment by moment walking of the eternal path of self-discovery.

5) In each moment, I have the ability to choose differently. As long as there is choice, there is hope and there is always choice.

The Soul's existence is experienced moment by moment, hence the term "momentum" because the Soul understands its eternal nature and how it creates.

When you build momentum, you are vibrationally building your moments, your eternal moments, choice by choice, sifting and sorting through your thoughts and choosing your path. This demonstrates the importance of being aware and engaged with your moment by moment thoughts and how you are building your path, through what means of momentum. It is either Soul based or contrast-based, those of the ego's presentations.

Contrast is a balancer. The universe is always presenting balance by way of contrast for the purpose of choice. There is always choice because there is always thought. When you acknowledge, then experience the different manifestations brought about by way of thought vibration, only then are you able to recognize your power to change. Your true power lies within your ability to choose and by this recognition, you deliberately create. When you turn your power of choosing over to that of your ego-driven momentum, you move vibrationally away from the path of your Soul. This too is a choice whether you acknowledge your power in it or not. You are always choosing your vibration through your thoughts and momentum which is the creating force of your eternal life, physical or not. It's all up to you.

6) In each moment, I am the perfect manifestation of my choices and I carry within me the opportunity to manifest myself mentally and physically in any way I choose.

Everything is energy vibration, beginning with your thoughts. Your thoughts generate a vibration and it is from that vibration you are "created" and are "creating."

Vibration is what creates the physical manifestation, as you are the physical manifestation of your Soul's vibration. You are the physical manifestation of the vibration of God and you are perfectly aligned with the vibration of your chosen thoughts. We emphasize 'chosen thoughts' because this is where you are first creating momentum and from the momentum, the experience is revealed.

We understand the human saying, "no one is perfect' and we say no statement is farther from truth for all are the perfect manifestation of their current vibration, 'current' being the operative word. Change is available, moment by moment in the rechoosing of your thoughts, and ultimately the choosing of your creating vibration. Your thought vibrations send out a signal of sorts to the Universe and are met with like vibrations which manifest into your physical reality. In order to change your current 'perfection', either internally or externally, you must change your moment by moment creation of thought vibration. In other words, vibrate your way to a new reality. It is all in your control. You are always living the example of your dominant vibration.

7) I am an aspect of God. My inherent vibration is the healing vibration of pure love and is accessible to me through my focus upon it. As my awareness of who I really am expands, all things are possible.

Jesus said, "All things are possible for him who believes." This quote, translated by us, means all things are possible for he who believes as his Soul believes, for from the Soul's perspective, there is no 'thing', no state of being, nothing that cannot be achieved through vibrational desire and agreement. Jesus exampled it and taught through his example.

Our human friends label his examples as miracles and to those who are out of alignment with the thoughts of their Soul and who are steeped within the contrasting thoughts of the ego, they certainly appear to be just that. However, all his works were examples of who you truly are. He walked as his Soul and demonstrated the power of choice as his own human aspect, you see. He exampled his focus for all human aspects. He demonstrated the God vibration within him through his healing and his physical creations. He taught, "Truly, truly, I say to you, whoever believes in me will also do the works that I do; and greater works than these will he do, because I am going to the Father."

Our evolved translation of this quote is, "Whoever believes in the example I am demonstrating through the vibration I hold, is capable of not only what I have shown but even more through your own consistent evolution and expansion of your Soul. I am transitioning back to the realm of pure love vibration and will continue to assist in your evolution, the evolution of the Soul of God, of the All, from a higher realm of being."

Many before you have taught of your power as the Soul of God, as the piece of the pie that is God and many will throughout your evolution. We say verily, verily discover who you are for that is the key to your salvation. It is in the knowing of yourself as a piece of the Universe. You are a manifestation of your Soul, that piece of God who chose to experience the contrast of the physical world in order to expand love either through healing or through joy. Whatever the chosen course, it is a necessary step in your evolution back to the pure vibration of love, of your Soul and of the Almighty Creator who is You.

THE TRUTH ABOUT KARMA

Our partner has included the common definition, stated below, of what our human friends call 'karma'. Karma seems to play a big role in the physical life experience and therefore adds to the fear of the collective consciousness of your planet.

When something or someone 'does you wrong' or there is what appears to be a 'stream of bad luck', karma seems to be the focus of the cause in many cases. You decide there must be a payback somewhere as to why this is happening to you and you throw up your hands and chalk it up to past life karma and you grit your teeth and hang on for the ride until this karmic payback has been satisfied. By accepting and allowing this old way of thinking into your experience, you are only perpetuating the vibration of it therefore re-creating it in each moment of focus.

So here is how one dictionary defines karma:

"• (in Hinduism and Buddhism) the sum of a person's actions in this and previous states of existence, viewed as deciding their fate in future existences.
• informal: destiny or fate, following as effect from cause."

As you can see, this definition sums up a person's life based on their actions. What we say is a person's life experience is based solely on their vibration.

Karma is an indication of an out of alignment vibration. It is seen as returning with you when you return to the third dimension and this is somewhat correct. However, it is not based on your actions toward another. Others can be involved of course, but the action needed to rectify the existing situation is not outward action but internal alignment.

The healing experience exampled by our partner in the beginning of this volume sets forth the healing process of the aspects and this includes, of course, what you deem your karmic dues. By re-aligning the aspect through the re-visiting of the last focused-upon vibration, the aspect is then healed as are all those who were affected by the manifestation of the misalignment. The process heals the aspect and the aspect is then free to move on to other timelines, leaving the "karmic bag" behind. This has a ripple effect on the journey of the Soul as the more aspects that are in alignment with the Soul, the 'easier' the journey so to speak. We would liken this to ten aspects in a canoe, all paddling the same way until one goes out of alignment. The continuing journey will not only be a struggle for the aspect who is askew, but for all aspects of the team as well.

Our partner likes that analogy as she has experienced the re-aligning within herself. Everything is vibrational alignment. Everything. You are the co-creator of your world, of your Soul's journey and as you become more and more aware of your role, as the human aspect, it is within your power to lighten the load, so to speak, by your focus upon your own alignment with your Soul.

We will sum up karma simply...karma is the result of an aspect who is out of alignment. The vibration that is out of alignment remains askew until it is focused upon again and the experienced perspective is changed from fear to love. Once the ending vibration is shifted and it is left in its dormant state again, it will remain in the loving vibration until it is re-visited, focused upon and reactivated.

CHOICE

All is chosen throughout eternity.
This universe is a choosing-based existence
where all evolution moves by way of conscious intention,
conscious choosing,
and therefore
conscious manifestation
which is accounted for and always
in perfect balance to itself
by way of vibration.

THE ANATOMY OF CHOICE.

All healing is based on choice. All, in fact, is based on choice. You are choosing in each moment, vibrationally, whether you are aware of it or not. This is why we are teaching about choice. It is the cornerstone to your existence.

When we say healing is choice, we mean whatever ailment or condition that seems to simply appear in your awareness and ultimately your experience, began in choice. Now that is not to say anyone deliberately chooses a specific disease or any type of what you deem as failure, however it is due to a vibrational alignment that is askew and the momentum that it carries. When there is manifestation of sickness, whether physical or emotional, the root cause, the beginning point is that point of creation which is in the choosing of the experience of any thought - which is the choosing of vibration, you see.

Our human friends, generally speaking, do not like this type of teaching simply because it seems to impose, in a sense, self-responsibility which of course it does, however this is the purpose of this teaching which is to expand your awareness of where you fit in the Universal laws. Our friend Maya Angelou said, "When you know better, you do better" and we agree.

This universe, as we've said, is vibrationally based meaning all creation, all manifestation is based on vibration. All manifestation is based on vibrational agreement and this includes the manifestation of a vibration that is out of alignment with that of your Source, your Soul. All manifestation that is not of love is indication of a skewed vibration. In other words, a choice for an egoic thought as opposed to choosing the feeling of the Soul. Your ego is a thinker. Your Soul is a feeler. We are encouragers of the vibrational choice that is always the one who feels.

When you live moment to moment, the momentum you are generating is easily increased in speed and intensity if you are present in each moment. If you are distracted from your vibration by way of any outside influence, your experience will reflect that of confusion, regret and imposition. In other words, you get in your own way.

When you begin consciously choosing your thoughts based on the way you want to feel, you begin to move into higher timelines as you raise your vibration. You create more opportunities to experience more love and expand your awareness and that momentum builds in the direction of self-discovery and living the experience of who you really are. This momentum leads you to the vibration of the New Earth. It is evolution at its best.

In Volume 1, we described the contrast and the presentation from the ego that creates the contrast which allows choosing. In order to choose, there must be options and when you are presented options, you are given choice. It is at this stage of the manifestational process that is your point of creation.

When you are presented choice, which happens every day, all day long through the conjuring up and focusing on your thoughts, you are offered an ego's thought of fear and the Soul's thought of love about the same topic, the same subject. You can picture yourself standing at a T. Perhaps if you choose the right angle, you are choosing with the ego, you form a vibrational agreement and the momentum begins toward a manifestation of the experience that choice will create. In other words, on any journey you have a choice of the back roads or the highway and each offers a different experience. Choosing your thoughts is a similar path.

There are many good things about having the ability to choose your thoughts and your experiences, not the least of which is your power to manifest. You see, when you give your power to someone or something else, meaning when you give your choosing ability away, you put your manifestations in the hands of other people or other things. This does not mean you receive what they are thinking and it does not mean you are not responsible. It does, however mean that that choice is made by default and the experience that that choice creates, will reflect the ego and not the Soul because the choice was made out of fear.

Each time you make a decision, each time you choose, you are, in effect, laying a brick down in front of your feet as you pave your own way. Each brick represents an experience you're choosing to have. The choices that form agreements with the ego go in one direction and the choices that agree with your Soul in another. And it's all your choice. You're building it as you go. There is no wrong way, only different experiences. Again, your timeframe is Eternal.

THE SOUL'S PERSPECTIVE OF THE HUMAN ASPECT

The Soul sees - feels - about its physical aspect as it sees - feels - for itself, the Soul aspect of you. Both are equal in value for all aspects are the true aspect of pure love and that is the natural state of being; It is the Collective You, of which you are an equally equipped piece. You, in essence, have a symbiotic relationship with Yourself. To put it simply, the true makeup of You is based in Love.

All your aspects, however many of them you are aware of - or not - are made of the same thing. It is our partner's vision of a pie, pumpkin is her favorite. No matter how thinly you slice the piece, it is made up of the same ingredients and each bite of a small piece tastes the same as the large. All bites, though, bring their own joy and the whole wouldn't be the same without a crumb, although they stand on their own, the pie and the crumb. We are making our point through an analogy because we understand the depth and width and universal size of this subject is humanly incomprehensible. We think our analogies work well for the scale we are referring to.

The human aspect, although equipped with the power of the Universe, sits in a realm of contrast, available to her upon her vibrational request. The Soul is emerged within the vibrational vapors of Love and sees no contrast, only love. The Soul is exclusively independent and the Collective One at the same time. This can get confusing so we'll give you the bottom line: The Soul sees all love, in all things, always. The Soul's underlying perspective is one of pure love and that's the reality where the Soul abides. It is always living. The human aspect is in the position to choose because of the contrast. If it chooses the perspective of the Soul, it lives as the Soul lives and is vibrationally sound in all thought. It is now available to all, the vibrational state of the Soul.

This is where we are heading, this shift of humanity. Everything is changing at once and it is being felt through manifestations of the bodies, minds and spirit. This is a loud call for the ascension of humanity. When Jesus rose from what you called death, he was exampling for all human aspects the power of vibrational transformation. He exampled his own physical ascension, because all ascend. Ascension is simply the natural process of evolution and there is not one thing that does not evolve. Jesus was one of those documented who changed the face of humanity as many before and after him. He is a teacher for the human aspect. He is a representative of Oneness. He is a pure example of Love and lived as his Soul on earth. In other words, he came to serve a purpose and he accomplished it. He continues to teach from a higher vibrational level, as you do and as all do, by example which is the example you set for yourselves.

It all boils down to how you see your own human aspect. We think you're pretty cool and without you, we would not evolve in this direction. The physical aspect of Us is as important to the collective Us as you, the individual aspect are to Us. The physical aspect allows the contrast for one reason and that is to expand the love vibration. We are the love vibration, you see. You are too; however, you have taken the opportunity to experience more aspects of Love, more 'ways' in which to feel love that is so the All of You can expand.

This is why it is important for you to consider your perspective before you judge yourself and to see yourself with the perspective of the Soul when you look in the mirror - inwardly and outwardly. See and feel yourself as the Love that you are and hold your standard in love only. Allow nothing less. For we are all the same, just seeing from different perspectives and we teach each other and we evolve together and we access each other and we live as One.

When the human aspect thinks less of him or herself, this is influenced programming from a source of skewed alignment in another, for your Soul never sees itself, any aspect of itself, as less than the pure love that it is. However, it stands in wait, so to speak, for all aspects to 'come home' vibrationally as when all aspects are in alignment, the Soul and all its components are a force of love vibration that create at a higher level.

In order to move into the New Earth vibration, all aspects must, we will say, rise to the occasion. They must, in essence, join forces - vibrationally - in order for all to experience the higher level of vibration that is now available. That is not to say if the human aspect chooses not to rise, all other aspects do not rise, for that is not the case. We are saying, though, when all aspects are in alignment with the Soul, the expansion is, well, more expansive. It allows a higher level of awareness for all, for The All of the Universe. We can liken this to a football or soccer or any team you are familiar with for you all know when all players, whether on the field or not, are in sync with the coach, with the quarterback or with the team leader, the team is stronger in their mission; they are more likely to reach their goal more quickly if all are working together for the same goal. This is the same for the Soul and its aspects.

This is simply seen through the example of the human aspect and the ego aspect on your planet. When the human aspect sees and works with it's ego brethren as it is purposed to, the human aspect will live as its Soul in the earthly plane, recognizing and choosing through the contrast presented by the ego. By this consistent choosing of love, the Soul, the human and the ego are all in alignment because they are all moving toward their purpose collectively, allowing the Soul to fulfill its purpose on earth which is the expansion of the Love vibration.

However, when the human aspect chooses the direction of the ego's contrast and the momentum is building toward fear, it is not in alignment with the Soul and is choosing another path that will lead to experiences created by the momentum of fear, not of love. These are manifestations of fear, struggle, confusion, pain and distress.

THE TRANSITION EXPERIENCE

This section is devoted to healing through what our human friends refer to as death. However, if you have read and experienced our first book in this series, you are aware there is no death as it is defined by your words.

Nothing 'dies' for all energy is only transformed into different vibrational states, different timelines and different experiential learning opportunities. All states of expansion, regardless of the state of the vibration, effect the All in a positive way simply because they are all fueled by love.

We define the healing process, whether it be emotional or that of your physical body, as the releasing of fear. When there is no fear present, no 'darkness' as some have referred to it, there is only light and no sickness, no despair, no conflict of any kind can be present therefore, all is 'healed.' This is the natural state of being of the Soul which is the eternal aspect of the collective You.

When the transition from physical to non-physical is experienced, all fear is dropped. The physical make-up, the body as it were, simply releases the positive vibration of the Soul simultaneously to the Soul's rising which is caused by the rising of its own vibration. That is the process, simply put.

Our partner experienced much contrast and much doubt from others when she became aware, experientially, of the ability to communicate with this vibration. She would say, "it comes with the territory." This is one of the opportunities when the awareness is expanded. Additional types of communication are available as the vibrational timelines are available as well. These are the timelines where some of your aspects reside.

As your scientists discovered years ago, energy cannot be destroyed therefore if you believe, as we've demonstrated throughout these texts, that you are energetic vibrational beings, you cannot be 'destroyed' either. It is a contrasting view provided and presented to you and many before you, as the death experience where, perhaps, there is nothing beyond your physical life on your planet or you go to a place where you are judged by others, namely God who has been personified through the teaching of others. Neither is the case. Our partner, open minded and sponge-like in her learning of who she really is, experienced this communication many times as have many, many others and as you are able to as well. This communication is the way to the healing process of grieving for those who have transitioned into another realm, yet they are available, vibrationally, upon your request. It is from the understanding of more that evolution happens and it is as natural as the consistent flowing of a river.

The teaching of fear in this arena is of the old paradigm of control manipulation, in the holding separate from who you really are. It is an attempt at the creation of levels of worthiness in a sense, and it is simply not universal truth. All vibrations are available to all those who desire to consciously walk the path of evolution and to experience all there is to offer in the way of the Soul. When Jesus said, "All things are possible for those who believe" he left everything to the power of the imagination.

You live in an all-inclusive Universe where vibration is key. To believe that one is more 'special' than another or 'gifted' in a way that is not available to another is the teaching of the presentations of contrast. It is not a teaching or an experience of the Soul and should be reconsidered upon your own experiencing of it for once you experience anything for yourself, there is no doubt left, for the light has exposed the dark and the dominant belief in a higher vibration is established. At this point in your journey, you are opening to new areas of awareness that are available at your request to all those who believe.

THE ENERGY OF FREEDOM

In this final section of the book of aspect healing, we want to discuss freedom.

Abraham taught "you are so free you can choose bondage" and in this statement, the bondage we are referring to is vibrational. As we've reiterated time and time again, everything is vibrational. Everything begins and (if there was an ending to anything) ends with vibration. All stories, all experiences and most importantly, all choices begin and end with vibration. Vibration leads to vibration which leads to momentum which leads to manifestation within you and with'out' you meaning the reality you create and experience through the manifestation of your thoughts. It is the premise with which you create your physical lifestyle and it is through your perceptions, your perspectives, your beliefs and ultimately your thoughts that this is so. You live outwardly what you expect inwardly - vibrationally speaking.

Healing is the result of vibrational alignment as we've demonstrated here in this mini-volume of statements and examples and analogies, all in the leading toward healing of maladies, physical ailments and emotional pain and discomfort. Healing begins with the knowledge of who you really are and frankly, what you're capable of - what your body is capable of - and alignment is key.

This is participating consciously within your consciousness. It is the recognition of the Oneness and your place within It, "It" meaning the Christ Consciousness of the Oneness of God. This is true authentic living.

Your body and your mind are capable of returning to who they really are, on a cellular level. That much is certain. The human aspect, through its choosing its way down the path, will either choose the Soul's perspective of love or the ego's perspective of fear and the manifestations that occur in the body and/or in the mind are directly related to those choices. However, as the human aspect begins to consciously choose the love vibration over the fear, the body and the mind follow suit and revert back to the natural vibration they held coming in, resistance is released and the mind and body are healed.

This exposes the truth of who you really are and when you are living the vibrational universal truth, this, our dear friend, is the Truth that will set you free.

OUR PARTING WORDS

We began this volume of the book of healing with the hope that all will consider a different perspective of the human aspect, the 'you' of this physical world. That perspective is the perspective of the Soul. It is the perspective of pure love. It is the perspective of the perfect creation of the God within you, the human expression of your Soul. This perspective is not based on a physical appearance. It is not based on your currency or your houses. It is not based on the weight, length or height of your physical vehicle. It is based solely upon your vibration and it encourages the natural and true vibration of your Soul to live through the human aspect, regardless of what others may assume or think about the human aspect that is 'you' for when you compare your human aspect to another, you are playing in separatism. You are responding to a vibration of fear of another's aspect learning and you are allowing your power of choice to be overridden by another's skewed vibration. This keeps you from alignment with your own Soul. It holds you apart, vibrationally, from where you chose to be when you arrived in this plane as a physical manifestation of your Soul.

We say this with emphasis and with strength of the knowing of who you are and that is no one can shift or manipulate or intercede with your vibration without your allowing of it. This is one reason we encourage vibrational knowing and vibrational strength in the knowing of who you are as a Soul. When you know who you are as your Soul, you will live as your Soul on earth. You will inhabit the New Earth not only on a vibrational level but as a physical being as well, experiencing for yourself the true Garden of Eden which is the manifestation of the pure love vibration in physical form.

We close this volume of work with a few quotes we have given to our partner over the years. They are snippets of information we hope will resonate with you on your journey forward.
We wish you well.

Namaste.

Quotes & Commentary
By Josef...

You See, The Light Is The Manifestation Of The Vibration That Heals And Where There Is Light, There Is No Darkness.

In a nutshell,

Anything you observe in the physical is a manifestation of a vibration. The pure vibration of love, that is to say the natural vibration of your Soul, is manifested as the purest of light. It is unseen by most humans in this form for it is the essence of whiteness...of lightness - and all around it, from a Universal perspective, is affected. This vibration is not seen through your eyes but is exampled through your focus upon it.

Just as the lower vibrational offerings of thought, by agreement with the ego's perspective, produce illness, or pain or emotional distress, the higher vibrations of thought produce healing for when the light is present, it alleviates the darkness, the lower vibration in this case. It is a rising above the vibrations of the lower realm and in that rising, all manifestations of darkness are 'left behind' so to speak.

All physical ailments, regardless of their inception date or time or place or specific seemingly "outward" cause are subject to healing as they are also subject to worsen through the momentum of additional and increasing momentum of lower vibratory thought vibration. All ailments, when exposed to the light, if you will - must subside you see for where there is light, there is no sign, no manifestation of the lower vibrations. It is law.

The Oneness Of
Your Soul
Is Made Up Of
The Love Vibration
Of Its Many Aspects.
You Are Its Human Aspect.
Your Ego Is Its Ego Aspect.
The Soul Is Your
God Aspect.
It Loves All Its Aspects
As It Loves Itself.
All Serve A Loving Purpose
For The One And All Are
Equal Parts Of Their
Collective Love Vibration.

In a nutshell...

You are multi-dimensional beings first. You are, as our partner likes to refer to you, as pieces of the same pie, all made up of the same energy ingredients and each as powerful as the next, and serving Its purpose in the makeup of the Oneness that is known to most of you as God.

All aspects of you are of equal value, you see. Most believe, by way of misaligned teachings, that this God you refer to is all powerful and omniscient and stands alone in Its sovereignty. This statement, although misleading on its face, is more true than not. However, the context must be shifted for it to be universal truth.

This God, this Collective Soul of the All, is powerful and omniscient indeed. This God, this piece of the Collective Soul of God, is within You, in all your glory and is the Collective Grouping of all your illusory individual and collective aspects. This teaching is new to most of our human friends and we are here to offer more understanding of it from your perspective simply because it is another 'puzzle piece' to who you really are.

The sense of unworthiness that many of you feel is taught into you by the old paradigm teaching that God is found outside of you therefore you must be less than. However, when you can view yourself as the Soul aspect of you, as the interactive non-physical piece of you, you begin to acknowledge and understand that you are that pumpkin pie piece of God, who retains the ability and the power to move mountains through your connection to the all-knowing Soul of you, who is God.

This God is the pure love vibration, the inherent and original makeup of your Soul, that evolves in each moment. The human physical aspect, by its agreement to incarnate at this time, serves this All, this Soul, this God, as It serves you, by agreeing through love, to expand - and by this choice, All agree(s) together with the intention to expand to a new vibration of Love; to expand the awareness of the human aspect where the All expands simultaneously.

This is true alignment with your Source, with your Soul. When all aspects of focus are in alignment, You are existing on the highest plane of consciousness, a different vibrational timeline if you will, that is always available to you.

Expansion is a choice and it is made in each moment. The power you have as an illusory individual human spans the All of your aspects and in each choice, you make toward love, the All eternally expands as One.

From Your Soul's Perspective, There Are No Mistakes, There Is Only Vibrational Choosing.

In a nutshell,

The word (and its connotation) "mistake" is a judgement. What is deemed by one a 'mistake' may be deemed by another a success.

The Soul's experience is eternal. All experiences that are presented to the human aspect are opportunities for choosing alignment. This is how the Soul 'sees' the experiences of the human aspect. Each time you choose alignment, which is the choice for love, you are expanding all aspects of the Soul.

The Soul is seeing expansion in each choice you make, regardless of the labeling of it, you see. Your timeframe for choosing is eternal. When Abraham teaches "you cannot get it wrong because you never get it done" they are explaining this quote.

Each choice you make, you are making vibrationally as well. You are choosing alignment with a vibration of fear or of love and each choice has an outcome that follows that vibrational pattern. In each moment, there is another opportunity to choose and to change, if you desire, the outcome of your vibrational choosing simply by choosing a different thought that carries a different vibrational momentum. As the momentum of the new thought alignment builds, the manifestation of that momentum creates a new reality and a new experience for you in the physical realm. Subsequently, all choosing of the Soul's perspective is carried with your Soul as it continues its own expansion at the eternal level.

To sum it up, your eternal life is comprised of experiences of choosing and all manifestations of your choices present more opportunities to choose and to create anew, if that is your desire. You are in constant motion forward in the expansion of your Soul's eternal journey by way of choice

Believing Something Cannot Be Experienced Does Not Mean It Cannot Be Experienced. It Does, However, Mean It Will Not Be Experienced By You. Examine Your Beliefs.

In a nutshell...

Jesus said, "All things are possible for he who believes." No truer statement has been said. Belief is a necessary component to spiritual expansion.

When you are in disbelief about something, anything, you are accepting the thoughts of the ego as your truth. Perhaps this belief is based on your own experience or the experience of others. However, the key to understanding the experience or the thoughts around the disbelief is in the understanding of the vibration and the momentum surrounding it.

If you believe, for instance, you will never have enough money or perfect health or the partner of your dreams, you are in vibrational agreement with the ego's offering of contrast. The reality that has manifested around any of these thoughts, beliefs if you will, has manifested because of the thoughts and the thought vibrational momentum. In other words, you get what you think about and focus upon. When you are consistently reassuring yourself of the beliefs you currently hold, you are building the momentum in that direction and you are experiencing the manifestation of the same.

In order to change your experience, you must change your thoughts about it which will change the vibration your thoughts carry and ultimately the momentum will shift to your new belief. Abraham teaches, "A belief is just a thought you keep on thinking."

If, for instance, you had been born in a different part of the world, in a different culture, to different parents, etc., you would have had a different set of beliefs handed to you during your informative years yet all humans are of the same Soul vibration of God, you see. It is in your choosing that you thrive; the choosing of thoughts, regardless of the circumstances or situations that 'are' in the current moment, for those things that are already manifested, as Abraham says, "are old news." They are manifestations, revealed through the vibrations they carried, and the beliefs that carried the momentum manifested as strongly as the belief itself.

You live what you believe you are capable of. You live what you believe you deserve and you live what you believe is possible ... for you. If there is something you are not enjoying about your physical experience, examine your beliefs about it and make changes in your belief 'system', if this is your desire. All is in your control and you are creating what you are living by your choice of beliefs.

When You Allow Your Soul To Lead, It Leads You To Your Alignment.

In a nutshell,

As you are presented with choice, by your choosing the Soul's perspective, you are choosing to Allow Your Soul To Lead you down the path of its - your - intended purpose. Your Soul always leads you toward more knowing of the love that you are.

Each time you choose your Soul's perspective, you are choosing alignment, you are choosing vibrational agreement with your Soul and by choosing this alignment, you then are positioning yourself, vibrationally, with all that the Soul has to offer in guidance, wisdom and knowledge.

Your Soul is the eternal non-physical part of you and is always focused upon you. As you expand your awareness to include the vibration of your Soul, that awareness brings with it all the possibilities of the Soul as well-meaning you, as the human aspect, have access to all the Soul 'knows.'

This is true alignment with the Universe, with God and with the Source of All that Is. By choosing alignment, you are choosing access and vibrational agreement with all you came in with, you see. Your alignment with your Soul is your key to an abundant physical life on your planet and this is the Soul's purpose. As the human aspect expands to include this vibration, it walks the earth as the larger part of itself, your Soul.

All Disease Begins & Ends In Your Thought Vibration. If You Remove Everything Externally That Is Said To Cause Disease, You're Removing The Leaves By Shaking The Tree. You Must Remove The Root, Which Is The Fearful Vibration, Or The Leaves Will Continue To Grow Back.

In a nutshell,

From the Soul's perspective, there is only well being; there is only Light therefore can be no disease. However, many on your planet are riddled with disease and discomfort and addiction, all due to a misalignment with your Source, or your Soul. Disease is a manifestation of the vibration of the illusion of separation.

When fear is released or understood for what it is which is an indication of this misalignment, healing must occur. A Course In Miracles teaches that those who want to believe in physical healing do well until the 'symptoms' don't disappear as quickly as they expect. However, the healing itself has taken place but as quickly as the fear re-occurs, the disease appears once again.

Your body has the ability to heal itself and when all cells are in alignment with their Source, healing must occur. It is the light that brings healing. It is only Love that heals and when Love is the dominant vibration, disease cannot be present within the body.

We see many cases of diseases that have been 'cured' in one area of the body, yet reappear in another. In these cases, and all like them, the leaves have been removed but the root - the fear vibration - continues to manifest.

You are a sovereign being of Light with the wherewithal to heal and to return to your natural state of being. Many on your planet have experienced this healing ability. They are not different from any other.

LOVE
HEALS.

That's It. In a nutshell.

Made in the USA
Monee, IL
29 November 2020

50035019R00049